BARBARA HOLLAND & HAZEL LUCAS

# Caring for Planet Earth

## THE WORLD AROUND US

A LION BOOK
Oxford · Batavia · Sydney

Text copyright © 1990 Barbara Holland and Hazel Lucas
This illustrated edition copyright © 1990 Lion Publishing

Published by
**Lion Publishing plc**
Sandy Lane West, Oxford, England
ISBN 0 7459 1350 4
ISBN 0 7459 2100 0 (export special edition)
**Lion Publishing Corporation**
1705 Hubbard Avenue, Batavia, Illinois 60510, USA
ISBN 0 7459 1350 4
**Albatross Books Pty Ltd**
PO Box 320, Sutherland, NSW 2232, Australia
ISBN 0 7324 0193 3

First edition 1990
Reprinted 1990, 1991
All rights reserved

**British Library Cataloguing in Publication Data**
Holland, Barbara
    The world around us.
    1. Environment
    I. Title      II. Lucas, Hazel
    333.7

    ISBN 0-7459-1350-4

**Library of Congress Cataloging-in-Publication Data**
Holland, Barbara.
    The world around us / Barbara Holland and Hazel Lucas.
    — 1st ed.
    ISBN 0-7459-1350-4 :
    1. Ecology—Juvenile literature.    2. Man—Influence on
nature—Juvenile literature.    3. Nature conservation—
Juvenile literature.    4. Conservation of natural
resources—Juvenile literature.
    [1. Ecology.    2. Man—Influence on nature.
3. Conservation of natural resources.    4. Wildlife
conservation.]    I. Lucas, Hazel.    II. Title.
QH541.14.H65    1990
574.5—dc20

Printed in Belgium

**Acknowledgments**
With special thanks to Mrs R. Hinton for her help and
advice.
Bible quotations on spreads 8 and 20 are taken from *The
Good News Bible* copyright 1966, 1971 and 1976
American Bible Society, published by the Bible Societies
and Collins.

**Design**
Graham Round

**Photographs**: from B & C Alexander 8 (left, above and
below); Aspect Picture Library/David Higgs 10 (left); Mary
Evans Picture Library 9 (centre); Fritz Fankhauser 20
(right); Sonia Halliday Photographs 9 (below left), /Mark
Nicholson 10 (right); Robert Harding Picture Library/S.H. &
D.H. Cavanaugh 17 (left); Hutchison Library 19 (right),
/Richard House 7; Frank Lane Picture Agency 11 (right);
ICCE Photo Library/Glyn Davies 12 (right); ICI 20 (left);
Lion Publishing/David Alexander 8 (below right), /David
Townsend 9 (above right), 18 (above right); Eric Marsh 13
(left); Milk Marketing Board 5 (right); Oxfam 14 (above
right), /Jeremy Hartley 18 (below left and right), /Peter
Wiles 14 (centre); Oxford Scientific Films/Doug Allan 17
(right), /Kathie Atkinson 3 (below right), /Henry Ausloos
15 (above), /G.I. Bernard 12 (left), /Stephen Fuller 3
(below left), /Muzz Murray 1, /Patti Murray 5 (above),
/Stan Osolinski 11 (left), /Charles Palek 2 (left), /Raj Singh
19 (left), /G.H. Thompson 5 (below), /Kim Westerskov 13
(right); Science Photo Library/CNRI/Tektoff-Merieux 6
(left); Zefa (UK) Ltd 20 (centre), /Kurt Goebel 14 (left),
/E. Hummel 4 (below), /Paulo Koch 14 (below right),
/Krohn 16, /Photo Leidmann 3 (above right), /Masterfile 4
(above), /M. Thonig 2 (right), 15 (below).

**Illustrations** by Peter Dennis 6 (compost heap), 15, 18;
Mick Loates 2, 4, 5; Denys Ovenden 1, 4, 7 (panda), 10;
All cartoons by Graham Round.

# CONTENTS

# MANY WONDERS—ONE PLAN

Our world is full of amazing plants and animals. Some live in faraway places, but many others can be found much closer to home. You could learn about living things all your life and never stop making fresh discoveries.

The plants and animals that are found in one part of the world may be very different from those that are found in another part. The reason is that different kinds are suited to different conditions. The soil and the climate affect the kind of plants that will grow, and these things in turn affect the kinds of animals which can live there. Each kind is called a species.

Each set of conditions is known as an environment. If you travelled around the world you would find many different environments. There are areas of grassland, forest, desert and mountain, all with their own wildlife, and no two places are exactly alike.

Each type of living creature makes its home, called its habitat. This might be a pile of old leaves, an area of woodland or a pond. The world has millions of different habitats.

In each one, the lives of plants and animals fit together like a jigsaw, all part of a wonderful plan. The sun gives heat, and light, which is used by plants to make their own food from carbon dioxide, water and nutrients from the soil. Plants are food for different kinds of creatures, large and small, and these in turn may be eaten by other creatures. All living things eventually die and are broken down into simple substances that can be used again. Nothing is wasted: everything is recycled as part of the great design. A group of species that depends on each other in this way, together with the surroundings, is called an ecosystem.

It is important that the ecosystem stays in balance: enough of each species must reach adulthood and reproduce. That way the species does not die out completely and each species can continue to play its part in the overall plan.

## AMAZING ADAPTATIONS

Some plants and animals have very special features that help them to survive in difficult environments. Wherever they live, they play their part in a complex ecosystem of living things.

### Beating the cold

Many plants prepare for cold weather by going to sleep. Some shed their leaves and others die back so that only the bulb or root is left, keeping snug under the soil. Some animals go to sleep too: they eat as much as they can before the winter sets in and then they hibernate in a warm den. Others grow an extra thick coat of fur.

In icy Antarctica Emperor penguins protect their chicks from

This simple food chain shows how the plants and animals in an ecosystem are linked.

Energy from the sun helps green plants such as this dog rose to grow.

A bee feeds on nectar from the dog rose.

A warbler catches and eats the bee. Many birds are omnivores — they eat both plants and animals.

When the fox dies, bacteria and other 'decomposers' break down the dead animal matter into minerals and humus. These enrich the soil so that plants will flourish.

the cold by keeping them on their feet, snuggled into their feathers.

## Getting enough food

Some creatures travel long distances to find enough food.

Elephants eat so much that they are constantly on the march.

The arctic tern flies from the lands around the North Pole about 18,000km (11,000 miles) to South Africa or Antarctica, depending on the season.

The camel protects itself against food shortages by storing food as fat in its hump.

And even onions and daffodils store food in bulbs.

## Doing without water

Camels can go for days without water. They get very thin, but can still work normally. When they find water, they drink gallons in just a few minutes, and soon look quite healthy again.

Desert plants such as cacti store water in their thick, fleshy stems or leaves.

## Outwitting enemies

Some animals hide from their enemies by blending in with their surroundings. Others run away. The skunk sprays a horrible-smelling liquid at attackers and porcupines roll up into a ball of prickles. Some plants protect themselves with spines or prickles.

The male Darwin's frog is a remarkable creature. It protects its mate's eggs from enemies by swallowing them. The tadpoles stay inside and hop out of their dad's mouth when they are frogs!

**The sundew cannot get all the food it needs from the poor soil in which it lives. Instead, it traps insects on its sticky pink petals and then dissolves them.**

A fox catches and eats the warbler. The fox is a carnivore that eats other animals.

## WHAT CAN YOU SEE?

If you have a garden, or live near some wasteland, mark out a square metre (yard) of ground and see how many living creatures you can find in it. Look below the surface and under stones as well as on top. Look in different weather conditions. Keep a notebook to record what you see. You may be surprised by what you find!

Make a poster of the plants and animals that live in your area. Find out what they eat, what kind of weather sends them hurrying for shelter, and how they protect themselves from enemies.

# FORESTS FULL OF LIFE

If you have ever been through a forest, you will know that it is dark and secret inside. Any plants that grow on the forest floor are ones that do well in shady places. They also have to be able to compete with the trees for nutrients in the soil. Forest animals can hide in the shady undergrowth and find homes in hollow trees. Forests provide a special kind of environment that is home to a host of living creatures.

## SHADY LEAVES

Deciduous trees are ones that lose their leaves each year. Before settlers cleared the land, much of Britain and Europe was covered with deciduous forest. Deer, rabbits, foxes and squirrels are among the many kinds of animals that can live in these forests. Numerous birds nest in the trees, and where the winter is not too cold they may stay all year, often feeding on seeds and berries.

The original forests contained mighty trees that took centuries to grow, but today there are very few areas that have never been cut for timber.

**Deciduous forests like this beech wood provide a home for many different insects, birds and mammals.**

## COLD FORESTS

Conifers can grow in cold regions where other trees cannot survive, such as parts of Canada and northern Europe. The trees grow quickly in the cool, short summers and keep their needle-shaped leaves for making food all year round. These leaves block out much of the light from the forest floor, and few plants can grow where the shade is very dense. Instead, the forest floor is covered with a deep, springy blanket of old needles. In winter snow slides easily off the narrow, waxy needle-shaped leaves.

Many birds nest in the towering trees, although only a few stay throughout the bitterly cold winters when the days are short. Some forest creatures — squirrels, for example — live on food from plants, such as nuts and seeds. Others, such as racoons and beavers, eat fish from the lakes and streams. Bears eat seeds and honey, but they also catch fish and hunt smaller animals.

**The American black bear will scratch trees and chew their bark to make other bears aware of its presence.**

# RAIN FORESTS

These thick, green forests grow near the equator. They have been less disturbed than other regions and contain more animals and plants than anywhere else in the world.

The trees in the forest like the hot, wet conditions and grow rapidly. Many of them have tall, straight trunks that rise some 30m (100ft) above the forest floor. The branches spread out at the tops of the trees to form a leafy roof called the canopy. Few plants grow in the deep shade, but where the sun can reach down the undergrowth becomes thick and impenetrable. This area of thick undergrowth is called the jungle.

Some rain-forest plants have solved the problem of finding light by growing on top of the trees. These plants are called epiphytes. Their seeds lodge in cracks between branches and grow there. Their roots may dangle down to catch moisture from the air, or they may trap water in their funnel-shaped leaves. This water also provides high-level ponds for tree frogs!

Elephants, tapirs, okapi and many small antelopes and deer are among the creatures that may be found in rain forests in different parts of the world. Large cats such as jaguars hunt their victims from the trees.

Many more kinds of animals live up in the canopy where they can find plenty of food. Small mammals such as flying squirrels and climbing mice make their homes in the trees, and many kinds of monkey can be seen swinging through the branches. Chimpanzees and gorillas are apes that live in the African rain forest, usually at a lower level than the monkeys.

Noisy parrots, beautiful birds of paradise and macaws fly around in the tree tops. The largest eagle in the world, the harpy eagle, lives in the forests of South America.

Powerful snakes curl around trees as they wait for their prey and huge spiders dangle from the trees. Beautiful butterflies flutter in the deep green light, and giant cockroaches scuttle in the darkness.

**From the forest floor to the canopy overhead, jungles are full of wildlife. In this South American rain forest are a howler monkey (1), an emerald tree boa (2), a hummingbird (3), flame vine blossom (4), a tapir and young (5), a macaw (6) and a *Morpho cypris* butterfly (7).**

# GRASSY PLAINS

Imagine a broad expanse of flat or gently rolling land. It is covered in tall grasses that bend in the wind, rippling like a green and yellow sea.

The great grassy plains of the world are places where herds of animals roam in search of pasture, and smaller birds, insects and other animals find shelter in the tall grasses. Meat-eating animals stalk their prey, and the victory goes to whichever creature is more cunning or can move faster.

## AFRICAN SAVANNAH

The great grassy plains of Africa are called the savannah. Zebras, buffalo, wildebeest, antelope and giraffes feed on the yellow grasses and the scrubby trees. Lions, leopards and cheetahs hunt these animals for food, and birds that eat carrion (dead meat) pick the bones clean. Life can be cruel for animals that are slower or weaker than others, but enough creatures survive to carry on the species.

The world's three largest land animals may also be seen on the plains or squelching in the mud by the waterholes: African elephants with long tusks and great, flapping ears, lumbering hippos and rhinos.

Cattle egrets follow where they tread to eat the insects these large creatures disturb as they churn up the soil. Tick birds ride on rhinos, feeding on the irritating little insects that lodge on the animals' thick skins. In these ways animals help each other to survive.

Antelope and zebra graze on the savannah below Mt Kilimanjaro. The herd gives some protection from the many meat-eating animals which prey on them.

## STEPPE AND PRAIRIE

The great plains of Europe and Asia are known as steppes. These areas generally have hot summers, very cold winters and little rainfall throughout the year. There are vast expanses of grass and some flowering plants, but trees grow only on the shores of lakes or along river banks.

Similar plains in North America are called prairies. These were once the home of vast herds of bison, but much of the land is now used for agriculture.

In the last century American bison, or buffalo, were hunted almost to the point of extinction. Today they are found only in nature reserves.

## AUSTRALIAN PLAINS

The so-called prairie dog is actually a burrowing squirrel.

Many of the creatures that live on the plains of Australia are unlike any others in the world. Kangaroos and wallabies are among the best known of Australia's animals, and they can bound along at great speeds.

This baby kangaroo, or 'joey', is able to feed without leaving the safety of its mother's pouch.

# HARSH ENVIRONMENTS

Some environments have extreme conditions—they may be very hot or very cold, or with very little soil. It is hard for anything to live. And yet, even in the harshest environments we find living creatures wonderfully equipped for survival.

## MOUNTAIN-TOP WORLD

The tops of mountains are colder than the lower slopes and some high peaks are always covered in snow.

In the Andes of South America, rare plants grow in crevices, sheltered from the wind, and eagles and condors build their nests on crags, safe from attack, and with a superb view of prey in the valleys below. Sure-footed llamas climb the ledges to find plants that other animals cannot reach.

## LIFE IN THE POLAR REGIONS

Can you imagine living in a land where for most of the year the ground is covered with ice and snow? This is what the regions around the North and South Poles are like. Polar animals face particular problems of finding food.

### The Arctic

There is no land at the North Pole itself, but the northerly tips of North America, Scandinavia and Russia and most of Greenland are in a region called the Arctic.

In winter it is very cold and the ground is covered with snow, but in summer it can be quite warm for a few months. Over a large area of the Arctic, called the tundra, the snow melts and grasses, mosses and small plants grow. These provide food for a large number of animals.

Some of these animals are summer visitors only, such as the reindeer, musk oxen and elk that come to find new pastures. Smaller plant-eating animals such as lemmings, voles and hares nibble on the leaves.

These creatures may be prey to the foxes and wolves that live in the area. The largest and most fearsome animal is the polar bear, which spends most of its life on the ice hunting for seals and fish, but it may also attack other creatures from time to time.

A large variety of birds live on the tundra, although many of them only stay there during the summer.

### The Antarctic

Antarctica is the name of a large continent at the South Pole. It has the lowest temperatures on earth—many degrees below freezing—and the land is covered with ice. In the summer small areas of ice at the edges of the continent melt and a few plants such as mosses and lichens grow.

The best-known creatures of Antarctica are the penguins. They often live together in colonies of many thousands of birds and they huddle close together to keep themselves warm.

The polar bear is the biggest and strongest hunter of the Arctic.

Air trapped between the feathers of these Adélie penguins helps them to keep warm in the icy water of the Antarctic Ocean.

### The polar seas

Although the seas in the polar regions are very cold, they teem with living creatures—many kinds of fish, seal, and whale.

The seals and whales are mammals and they have a layer of fat called blubber to keep them warm. The fish have a special chemical in their blood that prevents ice from forming in their bodies.

Fish and whales live on tiny marine animals and algae growing in the sea, and seals eat the fish.

# THE LIVING DESERT

Hot deserts are a very special kind of environment where there is very little water and large areas of bare rock and sand. The plants and animals that live here need to be specially equipped to survive without much water, and that is just what we find.

## Water-storing plants

All plants take in water through their roots and lose it through their leaves. Desert plants may have roots spreading for many metres (yards) around and below them to find enough moisture.

Cacti are special desert plants that grow in the deserts of North America. Instead of leaves they have spines, which do not let out much moisture. The cacti also have thick stems where they can store water. These plants burst into flower when rain falls, providing food for numerous desert insects.

## Beating the heat

One kind of desert tortoise burrows into the sand to hide from the heat of the day. In the burrow with the tortoise there may also be poisonous snakes, insects, desert toads or kangaroo-rats sheltering from the heat. Ground squirrels in the desert also hide in burrows.

The Gila woodpecker makes its home in a cool hole in a giant Saguaro cactus. When the woodpecker moves out, an elf owl may use the hole.

In this North American desert are three types of cactus — *Opuntia* (1), *Echinocereus* (3) and *Saguaro* (8), a burrowing owl (2), a gila woodpecker (4), a ground squirrel (5), a sidewinder rattlesnake (6) and a kangaroo rat (7).

# THE WATER SCENE

**Nearly three-quarters of the earth's surface is covered by water. Most of it is salt water in seas and oceans, but there is also fresh water in rivers and lakes.**

An enormous variety of creatures live in water, from the great whales in the oceans to tiny fish in the beautiful coral reefs that grow in tropical seas. To find out how some of these creatures live you could visit a pond, lake or stream, or the seashore. Each has its own miniature world.

## LIFE IN PONDS, LAKES AND STREAMS

If you visit a pond or stream and watch carefully for a few minutes, you can find many different creatures. Ducks and other water birds are often seen swimming about or sitting among the reeds.

In summer in some countries shimmering dragonflies or other flying insects hover over the water searching for insects to eat. In the water below there may be water beetles, water snails and different kinds of fish. You may see amphibians, such as frogs or toads, which come to the water to breed.

If you are very quiet you may see some of the furry animals that live in or near the water. These could be water voles, water shrews, otters, coypu or beavers, depending on which part of the world you live in. Most of these animals make their homes in the river banks, but beavers are master-builders and sometimes construct a home called a lodge in the middle of the river from twigs and branches.

In tropical countries much larger animals such as crocodiles and hippos live in the lakes and rivers.

The trees and plants growing around ponds and rivers are important to the animals who live there. Some provide nesting places and shade from the sun. Water plants help provide oxygen in the water for the creatures living there to breathe.

Insect-eating dragonflies are strong fliers found near inland waters.

Ponds like these are home to a variety of plant and animal life.

# LIFE ON THE SHORE

Very different plants and creatures are found on the shore of the sea or ocean. Some shorelines are sandy, but others are rocky. Each kind has its own wonderful variety of animal and plant life.

Exploring rockpools when the tide is out is a good way of discovering sea creatures. The sides of the rocks are often covered with sea-weeds. Lower down on the rocks you may see shellfish clinging to them, or even sea sponges.

In some places there may be sea anemones, which are really animals. When they are covered with water they unfold their tentacles and move them about to catch food. Life on the seashore is strange and beautiful.

Sometimes you may find small fish in the rockpools, or tiny crustaceans such as shrimps and prawns. Crabs often hide under the rocks or in the seaweed while they wait for the tide to come in.

You can also watch the many birds that come to the shore. Most of them come to catch fish to eat. You may see gulls wheeling and diving, and wading birds dabbling in shallow water.

If you see the sharp fin of a shark above the water, always come back to shore and warn other people in the area.

In some places you may see larger creatures such as seals and the dolphins everyone loves to watch. They are wonderful water-acrobats, seeming to enjoy every moment.

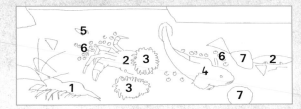

There are many seashore creatures to be found on temperate beaches. Here, herring gulls swoop across the shore and oyster catchers perch on the rocks. In the rock pool are a prawn (1), shore crabs (2), sea anemones (3), a blenny (4) and various molluscs, dog whelks (5), acorn barnacles (6) and limpets (7).

# THE MICROSCOPIC WORLD

Have you ever wondered why fresh food goes bad so quickly, why people catch illnesses from each other, or what happens to waste plant and animal material when it rots? For hundreds of years people were puzzled by these questions because they could not see the tiny microscopic organisms called microbes that cause such effects.

In the seventeenth century, a Dutch scientist named Anton van Leeuwenhoek invented a simple microscope that enabled people to see into this world. Today there are many kinds of microscope, including some specialized ones that can magnify objects up to 500,000 times their size! By using these microscopes we now know that there are millions of microbes all around us—in the earth, in water, in our bodies and in the air we breathe.

When we think about our world, we often think first about the large and spectacular things such as towering mountains, rushing waterfalls, exotic plants or curious animals. Many people, scientists included, look at the great wonders of our world and say: 'This could never have happened by chance. There must be a Creator-God who began and shaped it all.' The closer we look at things, the clearer this becomes: everything is designed, to the tiniest detail—far smaller than the eye can see. The tiny creatures in the microscopic world are just as interesting as the larger ones—and, like them, some are helpful to us and some are harmful, but they all fit into the Creator's web of life.

## MICROBES WHICH MAKE US ILL

Microbes that cause illness are often called germs. The most common kinds are bacteria and viruses.

Bacteria are very tiny creatures. Some are round in shape, like the staphylococci that cause blood poisoning. Some are rod shaped with tiny threads, like the typhoid bacilli, while others join together in long chains, like the streptococci that cause sore throats and scarlet fever.

Bacteria reproduce by dividing into two. Then the two daughter bacteria each grow to the same size as the parent before dividing again. In good conditions many bacteria can divide every twenty minutes.

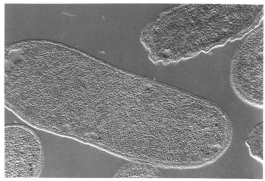

**These are salmonella bacteria, seen under a powerful microscope.**

Can you work out how many bacteria could be produced from just one in ten hours? No wonder we soon start feeling ill when bacteria enter our bodies!

Viruses are even smaller than bacteria but they cause many illnesses such as chicken-pox, measles and influenza. AIDS is a condition that is caused by a virus.

Because we now understand that bacteria and viruses exist, people try to find ways to stop them doing harm.

## PARASITES

Parasites are small animals or plants that live and feed on the bodies of other living creatures. The creature that is used as a home is called the host.

Not all parasites are microscopic: head lice that live in hair can just be seen with the naked eye. Fleas live on people's skin or in the fur of animals. Both these tiny creatures bite their hosts and feed on their blood, but although they are a nuisance they do not cause much harm in themselves and can easily be destroyed.

Some parasites are much more serious, however. The tiny parasite *Plasmodium* can live inside a person's blood and liver, and when it does the person suffers malaria. Millions of people catch malaria each year because infected blood is carried by a certain kind of mosquito from someone who has malaria to many other people. Malaria can be cured today by special medicines, but many people still die from it.

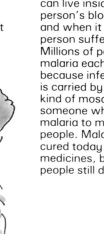

# USEFUL MICROBES

## A waste disposal service

Microbes help get rid of waste materials. Each day waste material is produced from dead leaves and flowers, animal droppings, the bodies of dead creatures and many other substances. Microbes, especially bacteria, and certain kinds of plants called fungi feed on this waste material. When they do, they break it down into important gases and minerals that go into the air or the soil and can then be re-used by living plants and animals. Just think what a giant rubbish heap our world would be if this did not happen!

## Making microbes work for us

Some microbes are very useful to us in making food or medicines. For these purposes people grow them commercially. The antibiotic medicine called penicillin comes from a blue-green fungus that grows on stale bread and fruit. It can kill some bacteria that are making people ill and so help them to recover more quickly.

Cheese and yoghurt are both made by mixing bacteria with milk.

Yeast is a tiny fungus made up of round cells that feed on sugar. When it eats the sugar it turns it into a gas called carbon dioxide and a substance called alcohol. Yeast is used to make alcoholic drinks such as wine and beer. When yeast is used in bread making, the carbon dioxide forms tiny bubbles in the dough that make it rise and give it a nice crumbly texture.

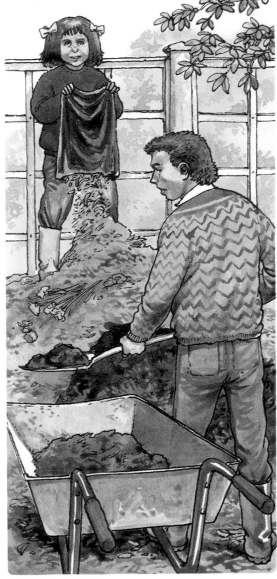

Some cheese has to be stored for months before it is ready to eat.

## BE A BAKER

Ask a grown-up if you can try making bread. Here is a simple recipe:

5g ($\frac{1}{4}$oz or one envelope) dried yeast
1 tsp sugar
150ml ($\frac{2}{3}$ cup) warm water
200g (8oz or 2 cups) bread flour
pinch salt

**1** Mix together the yeast, sugar and water. Set it aside until the yeast froths. It will take about 15 minutes.

**2** Meanwhile, mix the flour and salt in a mixing bowl and leave both in a warm place.

**3** Pour the yeast mixture slowly into the flour and mix together to make a soft dough. Add a little water if necessary.

**4** Knead with your hands for about 10 minutes.

**5** Put the dough into a greased baking tin and leave until it has risen to twice its size.

**6** Bake in a hot oven, 200°C/400°F for about 20 minutes.

If you try the same recipe without the yeast you will be able to compare the texture and see exactly what difference the yeast makes.

# A CHANGING WORLD

The wildlife in any place is suited to the conditions there, and all the species that live in that place depend on each other in some way. Any change will alter the balance.

Change can happen in different ways. A severe gale might blow down a lot of trees and destroy the habitats of all kinds of birds and insects, leaving them scurrying to find new places to live. A change in the weather pattern, such as a very long, cold winter might mean that few animals would survive into the following year. A volcano might erupt and cover a fertile valley with molten lava, ash and mud. People might decide to clear a forest in order to have more farmland or more space to put up houses.

If a community of plants and animals is faced with a change to their habitat, what can they do? Some benefit from the situation and adapt to it. Others may be put at risk. Sometimes an entire species may die out.

## HOW ADAPTABLE ARE YOU?

Think about the kind of home that you live in and the kinds of clothes that you wear in different seasons. Because you can think and plan, you can respond to change.

What changes would you have to make if the climate changed and the winters were much colder than usual and the summers were much hotter? Make a list of all the changes that you would have to make, or perhaps draw a picture of yourself and your new house and clothes.

# HISTORY IN THE ROCKS

If you look at cliff faces or other places where rock is left exposed, you may see layers in the rocks. These were created as bands of silt and sand built up underneath the seas long ago. The oldest layers are underneath the newer ones. Some of them have fossils in them—the remains of fish, plants, and animals that were buried in the mud.

A study of fossils in rocks of different ages shows that some species have continued to the present day, often changing their form to suit the changing environment. Other species have died out. Dinosaurs were once a very successful species. Suddenly they all died out. Some dramatic change must have made it impossible for them to survive.

## Which creatures will survive?

Although the plants and animals cannot think things out as we can, yet they are made with the capacity to adapt and survive.

The kinds of creature that survive will depend on the nature of the change. In general, however, those which exist in large numbers and breed very quickly will be able to adapt better than others.

Imagine that a kind of insect feeds on nectar in plants. In one year, because of the weather, only plants with long flowers grow well. Those insects which have longer tongues than others can reach into these flowers and so they survive while their shorter-tongued friends do not.

It is, therefore, only the long-tongued insects that live long enough to lay the next batch of eggs. Most of their offspring take after their parents and have long tongues too. Soon, all the surviving insects of that species will have long tongues.

Things might not work out so well for a creature such as the giant panda. There are fewer than 1,000 pandas in the world, and they eat only bamboo. If bamboo became scarce, it is unlikely that there would be enough pandas who could switch to eating something else quickly enough to survive. More probably, the species would die out and the world would lose a wonderful creature.

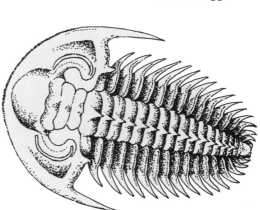

These fossil remains are of a trilobite. These animals lived in the early days of the Earth.

Much of the rain forest in Brazil (left) is being destroyed by people wanting to use the land for farming or to sell the timber. Care must be taken to protect the rain forest: it is home to a variety of wildlife and plays a vital role in regulating the world's climate.

It is important to protect bamboo forests which supply the main food of the already endangered giant panda.

Human beings are living creatures. They have many of the same needs as other living creatures. If they are to survive they need food, water and shelter; they must be able to reproduce and protect themselves from enemies. They need to fit in with various ecosystems that exist.

People are the same as other creatures and yet different. They are able to think and to feel. They are responsible. They can do some things that animals cannot do as well or even at all. They can talk to each other, work together, enjoy beauty and music. Why is this? What makes them special?

People answer these questions in different ways. One is through the creation story found in the first book of the Bible—the basis of Jewish and Christian beliefs. The world is brought into being by God. He makes all living creatures. Then the story goes on:

*Then God said, 'And now we will make human beings; they will be like us and resemble us. They will have power over the fish, the birds, and all animals, domestic and wild, large and small.' So God created human beings, making them to be like himself. He created them male and female, blessed them, and said, 'Have many children, so that your descendants will live all over the Earth and bring it under their control. I am putting you in charge of the fish, the birds and all the wild animals.'*

(Genesis 1: 26 – 28)

These words were written many centuries ago. As well as telling us that we should care for everything God has made, they say that people have been made to resemble God. And we alone can pray.

People have been able to use their higher intelligence to survive. They have developed clever ways of obtaining enough food and water, providing shelter in any weather conditions and fighting off enemies from other species. Different groups of people around the world have worked out their own particular patterns of survival. Here are some of them.

## LIFE IN THE ARCTIC

Today, reindeer continue to be herded in the traditional way in some parts of Scandinavia.

This Eskimo hunter has adopted a modern means of transport, but furs are still the best way to keep out the cold.

Several groups of people live in the Arctic. Their traditional lifestyles show how expertly they have adapted to the conditions of their environment.

In northern Europe, the Lapps built a way of life around the reindeer, which they herded and used to supply them with meat, milk, hides for shelter and clothing, bones and horn for tools, and power to pull their sleighs.

In the northern part of North America, several groups of Eskimos (Inuit) found other ways of living in a land of ice and snow. The traditional igloo was a shelter built of blocks of solid snow.

The Eskimo people built lightweight canoes called kayaks that they could paddle through the icy seas for transport. They learned how to hunt seals, bears and other polar animals, and used their meat for food, their hides for clothing, and their bones for tools.

Both the Lapps and the Eskimos developed a lifestyle that kept the natural balance. Some of their art shows their concern for the creatures they use.

Now that they have modern equipment they have the power to upset the balance. For example, with snowmobiles they can race over the snowy land and hunt more animals than before. If they kill too many, they put those animals at risk. In the short term they may have a much more comfortable lifestyle because they will not have to work so hard, but this could change their way of life for ever.

They are also threatened by people from outside their group who are beginning to use their land in new ways. For example, people are drilling for oil underneath the arctic seas. This industry, too, may upset the environment.

# LIFE IN THE RAIN FOREST

Different groups of people have made their home in the rain forests of the world. In these warm regions people are able to live in shelters made from branches, leaves and mud. They can collect edible plants from the forest, climb tall trees to find wild honey, and hunt creatures for their meat. Large leaves and animal skins easily provide all the clothing that they need for the hot weather. These people fit well into the overall pattern of life in their environment.

Today many rain forests are in danger; people want to clear the land in order to have farms. As the forests become smaller, the people and animals living there also are at risk.

## ON YOUR OWN

Imagine that you had to spend the summer alone in an area of countryside fairly close to where you live. You would only be allowed to use things that you could find naturally. Try to work out what you would do for shelter, what you could use to make special clothing, what you would eat and what you would drink.

# DESERT PEOPLE

Some people have adapted to life in the desert. Because plants and animals can only thrive where there is water, some desert people are nomads who are constantly travelling to find more plants for their herds of sheep or goats to eat. They live in tents that can be carried from one place to another, and they use camels, which are specially adapted for desert life, as a means of transport.

Other desert people have grouped around the permanent pools in the desert. A permanent pool is called an oasis. Trees can grow near the water and in some places it is possible to channel some of the water to grow crops.

These middle-eastern Bedouin families live in goats'-hair tents and move about in search of food and water for their animals.

## PEOPLES OF THE PLAIN

The native peoples who live on the great plains of North America used the buffalo to provide them with the things they needed to survive.

The people would hunt the buffalo and would then use the meat for food and preserve some for later. They used the hides to make tall tents called teepees that could be used as portable shelters. Softer parts of the hide would be used to make clothing.

Even though they hunted them, the Indian people had great respect for the buffalo. Before hunting, they would say prayers which reminded them not to be greedy when they killed other creatures. Their religion reminded them constantly to respect nature and keep the balance.

Today, these great plains are used mainly for farming, and the Indian peoples have had to adapt to a different way of life, although they still keep some of the old ways.

# SIMPLE MISTAKES

It would be easy to say that peoples who have a simple lifestyle cannot harm the environment. But sometimes they too make mistakes.

When European explorers discovered Australia they found people they called Aborigines, who lived mainly by hunting animals and gathering plants to eat from areas that were almost desert. Scientists now think that the land might once have been very fertile, and that the Aboriginal peoples might have been responsible for burning off the vegetation many centuries ago. If this is the case, then they made a serious mistake.

# MANKIND—THE MOST SUCCESSFUL SPECIES

Some groups of people have changed their environment a great deal. They have found ways to obtain all the food, water, shelter and clothing that they need, but then they have wanted more things.

Today, some people have managed to get so many things that they have a very comfortable life. But what is the cost? The more that people take out of the environment for themselves, the more they change the pattern of nature. If they take too much, they risk upsetting the balance.

The balance of nature has always been changing slowly, but as people have wanted more and more for themselves they have changed it very quickly and without realizing what they were doing. We are part of the natural world and must look after it. If we upset the pattern too much, we may even destroy ourselves. Somehow we have to find the balance that God intends.

## DOWN ON THE FARM

It can be quite risky to depend on gathering food from the wild: you might go hunting for animals and come back with none; in some years there might be few berries to eat.

One answer is to keep a group of animals behind fences so that they cannot get away. That makes sure there will be enough meat!

Another answer is to grow crops behind fences. These allow the specially chosen seeds or young plants to grow—safe from animals—until the crops can be used as food. Farming is a good way to make life less risky.

People began farming many thousands of years ago. While they only took a small amount of the land it did not upset the wildlife too much. Certainly, some kinds of plants and animals would have been affected, and these died out long ago. Even when the first parts of the Bible were written there were enough people farming the land to change the balance between species in the areas where they lived.

People cultivated new breeds of plant and bred new kinds of domestic animal to suit their needs. For example, there were cows that gave lots of milk, corn that had large grains, and lovely plump apples.

All this made life easier, so people had more time for other things. Some of them specialized in making nice clothes, shoes, carts, furniture, books, and so on. They were already changing the balance much more than people had ever done before.

In some places farming methods have changed little over the years. Riding an ox-pulled weighted plank is a simple and efficient way for this Turkish farmer's wife to break up the soil.

# A LIFESTYLE REVOLUTION

About 200 years ago, great scientific progress in the Western world brought many new discoveries. We call this period the Industrial Revolution. New machines were invented so that more products could be made more quickly. For example, people found faster ways to spin wool and cotton into cloth. Up till then, spinning was done by people who used spinning-wheels to produce one thread at a time. The new machines could make many threads at once.

Instead of sitting at home spinning, people went to work in the new factories where there were machines. Other machines were developed to make all kinds of other things. Steam trains carried goods very quickly to the people who wanted to buy them.

People needed power to make the machines work. Coal was mined from under the ground and burned to heat water to make steam engines work. Later, the steam was used to make electricity. People also discovered how to use oil to make machines work, and oil was pumped up from under the ground.

Many changes took place. The machines helped make life easier for some people, and supplied the needs of the growing number of people.

These people all needed food, clothing and shelter, and the many things that were being produced in factories. They began to take more and more things out of the environment: more land for farming to grow food; more of the coal that had formed underground from prehistoric forests; and more oil that had been formed at the same time. As a result, the pattern of nature was changed even more.

At that time the explorers from industrialized countries, such as Britain, France and Holland, were still discovering new lands, and they thought the world was big enough to supply them with everything they needed. Only as the years passed did people begin to see that they might use up the materials the world could offer them. Then there would be no more.

Shoppers in industrialized countries can be faced with a bewildering choice of purchases.

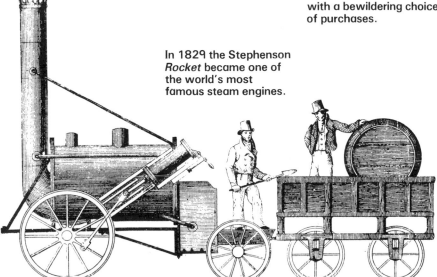

In 1829 the Stephenson *Rocket* became one of the world's most famous steam engines.

## CAN YOU SPIN A THREAD?

Before spinning-wheels were invented, people used even simpler ways to turn wool into thread. You can try the old method.

Get a lump of fleece (which you may be able to collect off fences or thorny hedges) and try pulling out a little bit. Twist this bit to make a thread. Tie your little thread on to something fairly heavy that will keep pulling out a little bit more fleece, and then set the weight spinning. See how long a thread you can get before it breaks.

How long would it take you to get enough thread to knit yourself a sweater? How long does it take you to choose a ready-made sweater?

# WILDLIFE IN DANGER

Our world has a tremendous variety of wildlife. Animals, birds and insects play a vital part in the land environments, and many fish and sea animals swarm the seas. Sadly, there is a danger that many species will become extinct. People today are making such great demands on the world's resources, and they have such powerful tools to help them, that many species are at risk.

People have always hunted and fished for food. Cave paintings show that some of the earliest human beings used spears and traps to capture their prey. It may be that the giant elk and woolly mammoth died out because the cave-dwellers hunted them so successfully.

Today, cultures that rely on hunting for food, and people who hunt animals for sport, have guns and can kill many animals very easily. Unless they cut down on the hunting, many species may be wiped out. People who go fishing can also cause harm. There may seem to be limitless numbers in the waters, but all creatures need to be allowed to mature and reproduce. If too many young fish are killed, the species will be threatened.

It may seem acceptable for people who really need food or fur clothing to go hunting, but some animals are hunted only to provide luxury goods. Many animals such as leopards, ocelots and foxes are slaughtered to make fashionable fur coats. Snakes and crocodiles are killed so that their skins can be made into shoes and bags. Elephants are destroyed so that the ivory from their tusks can be made into ornaments. Rare coral is collected to make expensive jewellery.

Another problem is that as people clear land for farms, factories and houses, many wild areas are lost. This leaves less space for wild creatures to live in. If they cannot find enough food in the area that is left, they will die. People can also spoil wild areas by dumping dangerous waste materials there. When God put people in charge of the world he made, they were meant to take good care of it. We need to remember that today.

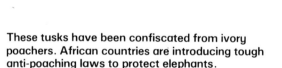
These tusks have been confiscated from ivory poachers. African countries are introducing tough anti-poaching laws to protect elephants.

## THE FUR TRADE

When European settlers came to North America, they found that some of the native Indians used beaver pelts for their clothing. People realized that money could be made by selling the pelts in Europe, where they were used to make hats. The fur was in such demand that beavers were hunted until there were very few left. If fashions had not changed, the beaver might have become extinct.

The beautiful fur of a leopard looks more attractive on the animal than as part of someone's winter coat.

## RAIDING THE SEAS

Every year more modern, efficient fishing boats are designed. They are very expensive and must be used to catch lots of fish every day if they are to be worth the money.

Modern factory ships catch and clean many tonnes of fish each day. Each boat has its own area for canning or freezing the fish, so it can stay out at sea for long periods doing this work. As a result of this unselective fishing, far too many fish are being caught and some species are in danger of extinction.

## DID YOU KNOW?

Once there were bears and wolves in Britain, and a variety of pouched animals in South America! Future generations may be just as amazed to find out that there were once badgers in Britain and kangaroos in Australia.

We need to protect endangered animals much more carefully or, one day, rare species that we can only see in zoos may not exist at all. In most developed countries there are conservation groups which will suggest ways you can help. Why not start by asking at your library for information on local groups?

## RARE BREEDS

People often think of wildlife when they think of species in danger. In fact, some kinds of domestic animals are at risk too. Earlier this century there were many more kinds of farm animals than there are today.

Most farmers have chosen to keep only the breeds that make a lot of money quickly: cows that give lots of milk, pigs that can be fattened for slaughter quickly, sheep with lots of wool, and so on.

The problem is that when breeders concentrate on making a particular kind of animal very efficient in one respect, the animals may be weaker in other ways. As a result, the breed may be more likely to get ill. It is important to keep a wide variety of breeds so that they can be crossbred with each other from time to time to keep them all strong.

Specialist breeders have ensured that these once-endangered farm animals are now safe.

Longhorn cow

Gloucester Old Spot pig

North Ronaldsay sheep

## PET HATES

The red-kneed tarantula is a giant spider that lives in Mexico. The species is in danger of extinction because people capture these spiders to sell to pet shops in North America and Europe.

The orang-utan is an ape that lives in the rain forests of Borneo. Many of this species were killed in the past because hunters killed mother apes so that the babies could be sold as pets. The hunting has been controlled, but now the creatures are threatened because their forests are being destroyed.

# INDUSTRIOUS PLANTS

Plants don't just grow to look pretty! They are vital to all life on this planet. Green plants are the only living things that can use the sun's energy to convert simple materials into food. As a result, they provide all the basic food that exists. We can only have animal products such as meat, eggs and milk if there are plants to feed the animals.

Plants give out oxygen when they make food. In fact, without enough plants in the world, there would not be enough oxygen for animals and people to breathe.

If plants are to grow well, they need the right kind of soil. In natural conditions where there is enough rain, the plants' roots bind the soil together so that it cannot be washed away by the rain or blown away by the wind. New plants quickly fill spaces that are bare. If people plough the land it does not have this protection.

The soil contains nutrients that are used by plants. When plants and animals die and rot back into the soil, the nutrients are put back. However, if a crop is cut and taken away, and nothing put back into the soil, then the soil will become exhausted.

Lush and healthy grass grows on a North American prairie.

## WILL THERE BE FORESTS TOMORROW?

Thousands of years ago, large areas of land in every continent were covered by forests. Over the centuries their leaves had fallen into the soil and helped make the soil rich. As people cleared the land for farms and cities many species died out because there was nowhere for them to live.

Many areas of deciduous forest were cut down centuries ago. Now woods such as oak, beech and ash are quite scarce and therefore they are expensive. These trees grow slowly so foresters are unwilling to plant them. If pine forests are planted in their place—as is happening in some places—the animals cannot adapt to the new environment.

Today, vast numbers of trees from the pine forests of cold areas are being cut down. Some wood is used to build houses and furniture, and large amounts are pulped to make paper.

The great rain forests which contain so many of the world's species of animals and plants are being cleared very rapidly. Some people are using machines to cut down the trees to provide farmland. But, in addition, the people of the rich countries are buying hardwoods like mahogany to make high quality furniture. The hot climate means that the land may be permanently damaged if these trees are cut down. Once the soil is cleared of the roots it is easily eroded by wind or water. The destruction of these great forests has led people to wonder if there will be enough plants left to provide the world with oxygen.

# ROBBING THE SOIL

Some crops use up a great deal of goodness from the soil. It is important not to grow the same plants in the same soil year after year. This mistake was made in the state of Georgia in the United States, where the once fertile fields used for growing cotton are now barren acid swamps.

In the American Great Plains states, settlers ploughed the prairies to grow wheat on the rich soil. After several years of drought, the soil dried out and blew away, leaving acres of dust.

A 'dust devil' whirls across an over-farmed prairie. Thoughtless use of fields can turn fertile farmland into dusty wastes.

## PLAGUES OF ANIMALS

Animals were first kept in herds in the Middle East. We read in the Bible book of Genesis that they caused problems even then! There was not enough grass in one area to feed the animals of both Abraham and Lot, so the two men had to go different ways.

In parts of Africa today, people keep herds of cows, sheep and goats. Cows eat the sweetest grasses down to the ground, causing the soil to dry out. Sheep can nibble very short, coarse grass, and goats eat young shoots and trees and pull grass up to get at the roots.

Too many animals on poor soil may kill the grass completely so that it does not grow again. The hot winds can then blow away the topsoil, and the area becomes a desert. Domestic animals, people and wildlife may all starve. Overgrazing is making the deserts of the world larger every year.

## PLANT A TREE!

Perhaps you would like to grow some trees of your own? It isn't very difficult to grow tree seedlings — you can try different seeds to see which kinds grow best.

Large hard seeds should be sown fresh, but some varieties germinate better if they have been kept cold for a while. A margarine tub in the bottom of the refrigerator, just above freezing, will do nicely!

After a few weeks, plant the seeds in a pot of soil kept in a cool place. Small seeds should be placed close to the surface and larger ones deeper in the pot. Water the soil and cover the pot with a plastic bag to stop it drying out.

You will need to be patient, as the tree seedlings may take several weeks to come up. When they are large enough to plant outside, they will still need protecting from animals and you will need to water them in dry weather.

Remember to find out how big your trees will grow, and plant them where there is enough room!

The rocks from which our planet is made contain many valuable substances. It is costly and often dangerous to mine the rocks, but the substances are so useful that people think it is worth the trouble to get them. They often forget, however, that there is a limited supply of minerals. Once they have been dug out, they are gone. Today, people can mine so efficiently that there is a real risk that we will use up some minerals completely.

## FOSSILIZED FORESTS

Many thousands of years ago prehistoric forests covered our planet. The old trees fell into swamps and were eventually covered by layers of soil. The wood was squeezed so hard by the layers on top that it changed and became a different substance: coal!

It took thousands and thousands of years to make the coal, and yet large amounts of it have been dug out and burned in the last 200 years. It is used to power steam engines and to make electricity. Some of it is used to provide chemicals for other purposes such as soap (yes, really). Although there is still a lot of coal left, the supply cannot go on for ever.

One day the supply of coal from this huge mine in Zimbabwe is sure to run out.

# BLACK GOLD

## NON-RENEWABLE RESOURCES

Imagine that someone leaves you a large sum of money—perhaps ten thousand times what you might be given as a birthday gift! You have never been so wealthy. You could go out tomorrow and buy all the things you were saving up for. You could have parties for all your friends every week and could afford to give them lots of treats.

But wait: when you have spent the money, it will all be gone. No one is going to give you any more. If you spend it on things that are really important, you will be able to enjoy it and it will probably last quite a long time—perhaps until you are grown-up and able to find another way to make money. If you spend it on silly things you will not benefit from it as much, and you may spend it more quickly than you thought.

Minerals such as coal and oil are like a gift of great wealth, but it is only given once. People need to learn how to use it wisely, and make it last.

Oil is sometimes called black gold because it is so valuable. Oil was also formed many thousands of years ago when the remains of masses of sea creatures were squeezed under the layers of rock that covered them. The oil can be used as a fuel for all kinds of machines, and a special type of refined oil is used to make fuel for cars.

The chemicals in oil have many other uses. They can be used to make synthetic fabrics and many kinds of plastic. Like paper, plastic goods are often used once and then thrown away. Yet we use so much oil that we risk using up all that there is.

Also, unlike some waste, most plastic cannot be recycled. Why not see if you can reduce your family's use of plastic? One way is to buy products with less packaging. Can you think of others?

**These plumes of air-polluting flames and smoke are the result of an oil well blow-out in Kuwait.**

# A TERRIBLE WASTE

Does your room look like a dump? Only sometimes, you say! Imagine what it would be like to live on a real waste dump. Not only would it be messy to look at, but it would be smelly, dirty and dangerous. The problem today is that there are so many people in the world and so many things to be got rid of that the entire world is turning into a waste heap.

## IS THE WATER SAFE?

Clean water to drink is essential to life. But much of the world's water is very polluted. The River Rhine in Germany is particularly badly polluted by chemicals from the nearby factories.

Sewage is often tipped into rivers or the sea. It contains many bacteria. Sewage needs to be treated to kill these germs or people may become ill from drinking contaminated river water.

Oil spilled from oil tankers and offshore oil wells is a problem. The oil kills many fish, sea-birds and other sea creatures. If it is washed ashore it can ruin beaches.

## THE AIR WE BREATHE

To stay healthy we need to breathe clean air. In many industrial areas, however, the air contains harmful substances. Factories and power stations pour out smoke and gases that can damage our lungs.

Cars and other vehicles send out poisonous substances in their exhaust gases which can damage our brains or have other unpleasant effects.

Plants, too, are affected by polluted air. The sunshine cannot

## TO THE DUMP

### Household waste

Have you ever wondered where the waste that you throw out goes? Some of it, such as waste food and vegetable peelings, will decay on the dump where it is left. The materials it is made of will then be used again. This kind of waste is called bio-degradable. Recycling, or re-use of materials, is part of the plan built into the natural world.

Other kinds of waste material cannot be broken down in the same way. These include most of the plastic containers and cans that human beings make and then throw away, and larger items such as old beds and TV sets. It would be possible to use some of the materials again, but often the process is costly and so these things may be just thrown into rivers or lakes or dumped in fields and woodland.

### Industrial waste

Industries also have waste to get rid of. Sometimes their waste contains dangerous chemicals.

### Radioactive!

Nuclear reactors provide a way of making electricity. The problem is that the materials left over after making the electricity become radioactive. This means that they give off invisible radiation that can kill body cells or cause cancer. Some of this waste needs to be encased in concrete and stored for thousands of years. Dangerous substances would leak out if the concrete cracked, and could damage living things.

The safe disposal of domestic waste is a growing problem throughout the world.

reach them through the smoke and gases, and the dust that settles on their leaves may prevent them from breathing properly.

In recent years people have burned so much fuel for their homes, factories and cars that the amount of carbon dioxide in the air has increased. Carbon dioxide is not harmful in itself, but too much of it causes a problem.

There are now also fewer trees to convert the carbon dioxide back to oxygen. The gas forms a layer in the atmosphere that prevents heat escaping. This layer acts like glass in a greenhouse. The result could be that the Earth will get much warmer. It might even melt the polar ice and cause seas to rise. Land would be flooded and people could lose their homes. This is called the 'Greenhouse Effect'.

## Acid rain

Some of the gases that are found in the smoke from power stations and factories mix with water vapour in the air. When the water falls as rain, the chemicals make the rain acid. When this acid rain falls on lakes and rivers it kills the plants and animals there. It also damages trees and buildings. In Canada, the United States, Sweden, Germany and many other countries, acid rain is killing forests and lakes.

Waste gases from industry do not cause only local pollution. The waste from industrial nations causes problems for people everywhere.

## KILLER SPRAYS

Sometimes people spray the land with dangerous chemicals. Insecticides are used to kill insect pests and strong weedkillers are used to stop unwanted plants from choking crops. These chemicals may also kill other animals and plants. They may even get washed into our own water supply.

## HOW BIG IS THE PROBLEM?

Keep a chart to record how much waste your family throws away each week for 4 weeks. Think what a problem it would be if you had to keep the waste! Where would you put it? *What would it smell like?*

But the things you throw away may sometimes be useful. Waste food can often form part of a compost heap, eventually returning goodness to the soil. Many other waste items can be recycled (see spreads 15 and 16).

# RICH AND POOR

People today use many of the world's resources greedily, but not only plants and animals are at risk. Another problem is that only *some* of the people benefit from the way the world is being used. Many others are left desperately poor. They do not have enough food. They do not have clean water. They have so few clothes they may not even have enough to keep them warm. They may have shabby houses or none at all. We risk letting members of our own species die in misery because we are acting selfishly.

## WATER ON TAP

Most of the water you drink comes out of a tap (faucet). You use it for baths, to get your clothes clean, and to drink. Most of us waste gallons of clean water every day.

In poor countries people may have to walk many miles to get a pot of water. When they find it, the water may be dirty and dangerous to drink, and they may have to use the same water for washing, drinking and cooking.

Water Aid, Tear Fund and SIFAT are just a few of the many international relief agencies working to bring fresh water to isolated communities throughout the world. They offer help in locating water and drilling wells which can transform the lifestyle of many families.

### TRY THIS!

Fill up a bucket of water and see how far you can carry it before you decide it is too much bother and want to tip it away. Imagine what it would be like if you had to walk twice as far for all the water you used in a day. Do you think that you could balance it on your head?

In some places a supply of fresh water cannot be guaranteed. Here a visit to the well has proved worthwhile.

## LIFE IN A CARDBOARD BOX

Sometimes it can seem unbearable to have to share your bedroom with a brother or sister! In some poorer countries, people from the country areas realize there is no more room for them to farm the land. They flock to the towns to look for other work. Many of them will not find it.

On the outskirts of some cities, the poor people live in shanty towns. They have no clean water and no proper drainage for toilets. A whole family may share one room — they are all crammed together in makeshift shelters made from scrap materials and cardboard boxes.

These ramshackle huts in Hong Kong are the homes of many families.

## OPEN YOUR MOUTH AND SAY 'AARGH!'

Few people really enjoy visiting the dentist. It isn't a real thrill to go to the doctor either, particularly if you need an injection. In poor countries people don't have this problem. They probably don't have the chance to see either a doctor or a dentist. . . Instead, if their teeth hurt, they either put up with the pain or have their teeth pulled out by someone who may not even be trained and who has no pain-killers.

Unlike you, children are not given injections to prevent disease and many die of simple illnesses that doctors all over the world know how to prevent. The problem is that there isn't enough money to pay for the right sort of care.

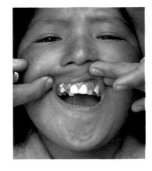

**In many parts of the world a visit to the dentist is a privilege!**

## WORKING FOR THE WEALTHY

Many people in poor countries work very hard indeed, but earn very little money in return. Some of them are making goods that people in the wealthy countries want.

No wonder those imported jeans are so cheap! And that splendid computer: people in a poor country may have strained their eyes to assemble it, even damaging their eyesight.

**In some countries factory workers are well paid, in others they may earn barely enough to live on.**

# RECLAIM THE WORLD

So far we have not looked after God's world at all well. Can anything be done to restore the balance? God gave us brains and intelligence which we can use in good ways or in bad ways. We can choose, too, to live selfishly, or to share with others and care about them. Now that we know how and why the balance of nature is upset, we can go about putting things right.

The animals and plants that we use will renew themselves naturally if we let them grow and reproduce. We can still take some plants and animals to meet our needs—perhaps not as many as before, but still enough—and we can make sure that species have a good chance of continuing to thrive, rather than dying out.

## SAVE THE ANIMALS

It is time to think hard about the animals that people are allowed to hunt. It would be very sad to lose species just for the sake of a fashion trend, and their extinction might upset the balance in the environment more than we think.

Once zoos had a bad name for taking wild animals and displaying them as freaks. Now they can play a helpful role in preserving highly endangered species, breeding them in protected conditions, and returning some to the wild. This scheme has already worked for some species, such as the Arabian oryx with its graceful curving horns, and the American bison.

It is also possible to set up nature reserves in the wild and make sure that the creatures that live in them are left to themselves.

The rare Przewalski's horse found in Mongolia is the only truly wild relative of domestic horses. Some of these animals are now kept in zoos to ensure the survival of the breed.

## PUT BACK THE TREES

People have been cutting down forests at a tremendous rate. It is time to slow down the amount of cutting down and to plant trees to replace the ones that we do use. That way, people can still enjoy the things that are made from wood without damaging the environment.

As so much wood is used to make paper, it is worth using paper more than once. You can use the clean side of used writing paper for drawings and craft work. You can give waste paper to people or organizations that will recycle it and in that way you can save trees from being cut down.

## FARMING WITH CARE

Farming can work in harmony with nature, not against it. It is important for people to vary the crops that they grow on a piece of land so that they do not exhaust it. They can cut down on the use of chemicals so that they do not poison the environment. They can take care not to leave land bare so that the soil does not get washed away.

Changes in animal farming could be helpful, too. Many farm animals are kept in crowded conditions indoors and fed artificial feeds. Perhaps it would be better if the animals could live in the open and eat the kinds of food that kept their wild ancestors healthy.

We could also find new foods for all the people in the world. Some kinds of seaweed can be used to make foods that are nutritious. Special fungi can also be used to supply protein, and the result could be even more delicious than mushrooms! Beans can also be used to make products that could replace some of the meat people eat.

Farmers can grow healthy crops without using so many chemicals, but they may also harvest a few more wild flowers!

## SAVE THE FISH

Fish lay millions of eggs, so their chances of building up their numbers if we cut back on fishing are very good. Governments are now making laws setting limits to the number of fish that may be caught. There are other laws saying that nets must have a large mesh that will allow younger fish to slip through.

In some places fish farms have been set up. Little fish are grown in ideal conditions so that they quickly reach a good size. Fish farms provide enough for people to eat without taking wild species.

## YOUR OWN LITTLE PATCH

If you have a piece of ground at home or at school, you can think about ways to use it well. Perhaps you could plant a tree. You might prefer to grow vegetables and learn about how to grow different ones on different parts of the garden each year so as not to wear out the soil. Or you could let some of the land go wild so that it becomes a little nature reserve.

Minerals that we take from the ground can never be replaced. Once they are gone they are gone for good. What we can do is to make sure that we do not waste them. Often we can find ways to use minerals more than once.

## RECYCLING

Not everything we throw away is useless. Other people may be able to put some of your waste materials to good use.

Paper (see spread 15) is only one of a number of materials that can be recycled quite easily.

Some communities have schemes for collecting glass bottles. The glass can be crushed and then processed to make new glass.

Metal is easy to recycle because it can be melted down and used to make a new metal object. In fact, it takes less energy to melt scrap metal than to process metal ore. There are schemes to collect aluminium, copper and lead. Be careful with lead, as it is poisonous.

Perhaps you could persuade your family to start taking these useful waste materials to the special collection places found in many towns.

If your family owns a car, think about ways to keep it running for as long as possible. Many people scrap their cars so they can have a glamorous new one, but keeping an old one going saves the world's resources.

When you are buying writing paper and wrapping paper, try to buy paper that has been recycled. Some of it is very attractive.

Cars are piled up in a scrapyard. Some of the metal in these old cars can be melted down and reused, but many waste materials will remain.

# CUT DOWN ON WASTE

Avoid using products that damage the environment. If you have a choice, try not to use disposable plastics that will simply pile up on waste dumps. They may take 200 years to break down!

Gases called chlorofluorocarbons (CFCs), which are found in aerosols and refrigerators, damage the Earth's atmosphere. They break down the ozone layer—a layer high above the Earth that shields us from the ultraviolet light of the sun. Too much ultraviolet light may cause skin cancer, affect the growth of crops, and alter the weather.

Avoid using aerosols that damage the atmosphere. There are other kinds of sprays that work just as well.

When you shop, look out for labels on products which show they do not damage the environment. Then try to persuade your family and friends to buy these items instead of others which may be harmful to the world around us.

High in the atmosphere the ozone layer protects the earth from the sun's dangerous ultra violet rays. Gases called CFCs are gradually destroying this layer and many countries are now limiting their production.

sun

sun's ultraviolet rays

ozone layer

hole in ozone layer

Earth

## WASTED ENERGY

People burn up a lot of oil and coal just keeping their homes warm. It is a good idea to stop heat escaping so that you stay just as warm but use up less fuel. Perhaps you could remind your parents that insulating your roof and stopping draughts are two ways to do this.

It is also a waste of fuel to insist on going in a car to places that you can reach in other ways. Perhaps you could walk or cycle. Perhaps you could go on a bus or train. If you need to go by car, perhaps you could take someone else with you who wants to go to the same place.

Today, there are many people in the world, and they all want energy. What kinds of energy does your home use? If you live in a developed country, one important kind will be electricity. Try to imagine how your life would change if everything electrical in your home suddenly disappeared! What would you miss most?

Think further afield. What energy do your parents need at work? Many factories would stop production without fuel or electricity. Workers would be sent home and, with nothing to sell, shops would close. With no petrol or gasoline, cars, trucks and tractors would be useless.

At the moment, most of our electricity comes from oil- or coal-fired power stations, or from nuclear energy. These use minerals that cannot be replaced, but we shall still need them for many years to come. It is worth developing sources of energy which may take their place one day.

## SOLAR POWER

Heat from the sun is a kind of energy which can sometimes be used directly.

There are also ways of focusing the sun so that it heats water. This heat is used to create steam to turn turbines, and the turbines make electricity.

In addition, some countries are now experimenting with beaming solar energy in from space, reflected from satellites!

## RUSHING WATER

Water can be used to turn special wheels called turbines to make electricity. Hydro-electric power, as it is called, is already used in places that have natural waterfalls. Countries such as Canada, Brazil, Norway and Sweden use this form of electricity a great deal.

Often the waterfalls are managed so that some water is diverted to make electricity. In fact, the mighty Niagara Falls only gush at full force during the day; at night some of the water is channelled to the hydro-electric power station!

Where there are no natural waterfalls, people can sometimes create a hydro-electric power station in mountainous areas by building a dam across a river. The water is allowed to fill a reservoir behind the dam and then it is released to turn the turbines. The only problem is that beautiful valleys are lost when reservoirs are made.

The tides may also be a source of power. Some tidal power stations have been set up. The water races in through the turbines to make electricity.

## WIND POWER

Windmills have been used for centuries to capture the energy in the wind. Modern windmills can be even more efficient and can supply small communities with all the electricity that they need. However, you need vast areas of enormous windmills to replace one ordinary power station!

## NUCLEAR FUSION

The nuclear power that is currently produced depends on splitting atoms. This is called nuclear fission. Nuclear fusion (the opposite of nuclear fission) is a very complex process, but it offers hope of producing lots of cheap electricity with much less problem of radioactive waste.

**Waterfalls can be both beautiful and useful if they are harnessed to produce hydro-electric power.**

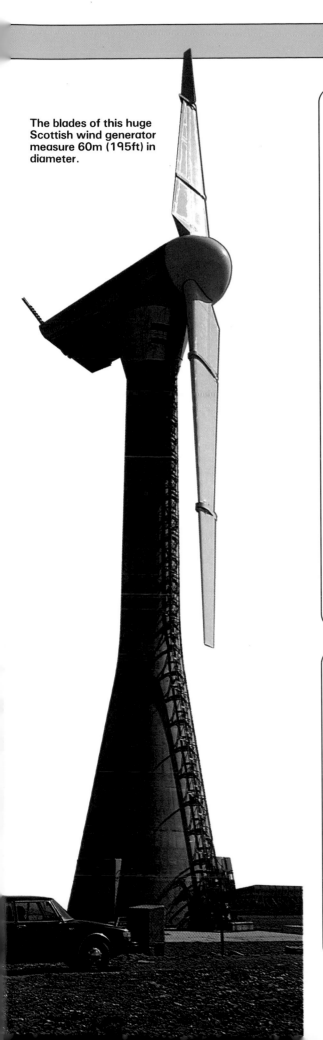

The blades of this huge Scottish wind generator measure 60m (195ft) in diameter.

## DON'T POOH-POOH BIOGAS

A few years ago, Indian villages were facing a crisis. Firewood, the traditional fuel, had almost run out, and the children who collected it had to walk all day to find any. Richer families who owned pigs began to burn the dung as fuel, but the pig dung was usually used as fertilizer, and without it the fields grew fewer crops.

A group of Indian scientists worked with the villagers to produce a biogas digester. This is a tank where dung (usually from pigs) decays. As it does so, it gives off a gas called methane, and this gas can be used for cooking.

The tank was too expensive for one family, but the village could share one. Those who owned a pig put in pig dung, and other people brought all kinds of household waste. There was enough methane for everyone, even those who were too poor to own pigs.

After it had decayed, the residue was still good as a fertilizer for the fields. The children could go to school because they did not have to fetch firewood, and the trees were left to grow.

Many villages in India have been helped by this invention, and a similar one has been used in China.

## DRINKING AND DRIVING

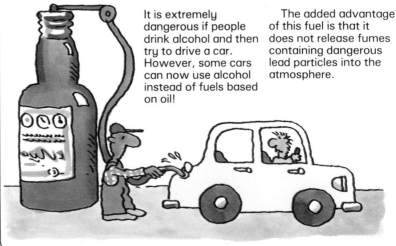

It is extremely dangerous if people drink alcohol and then try to drive a car. However, some cars can now use alcohol instead of fuels based on oil!

The added advantage of this fuel is that it does not release fumes containing dangerous lead particles into the atmosphere.

# HEALTHY AND HAPPY

Human beings are doing very well as a species. Over the last 200 years the number of people living in the world has increased many times. One reason is that people have learned how to keep healthy. They have found ways of curing many illnesses and of preventing people from getting some dangerous diseases. Improvements in medical care are good, but more need to be made.

## GETTING CROWDED

Our world is at risk partly because there are so many people. We cannot find extra room on the Earth, nor can we send a few million people to another planet. All we can do is to make sure that our families are small, so that the numbers don't go up any more.

In the rich countries people can be confident that their babies will live, and so they are happy to have just a few children. In poorer countries people still have many children so that they can be sure that enough will survive to help them with the hard work of fetching water and gathering firewood. Later, the children will be there to look after the parents when they are old. If these people can have better health care, they can safely have fewer children if they wish.

## FOOD FOR THOUGHT

At the same time that people in the wealthy countries have often forgotten to take care of the world, they have forgotten to take care of their own bodies. Many of them eat too much, and too many foods that are bad for them.

It is really sad to think that some people are unhealthy because they eat too much while other people are unhealthy because they do not have enough.

Another way to make the world a better place to live in is to be less greedy about food. People who have a lot could eat more simply so that they could share more with people who have less. Why should wealthy people have meat and potatoes and vegetables *and* dessert when poorer people have only rice?

Why don't you and your family talk about what you eat? By small changes to your diet, or helping to plan menus more carefully, you could help use the world's food resources better.

In countries where food is scarce, relief organizations may sometimes give seed to farmers so that they can grow a healthy food crop in the year ahead.

This simple modern well has given these African villagers a fresh, clean water supply near to their homes.

## THE HEALTH VISITOR

It is possible to prevent many diseases if babies are given the right injections, and it is possible to cure many illnesses quite simply. In some poorer countries people are training health visitors to do this kind of work, so that the few doctors who are available can deal with people who are more seriously ill.

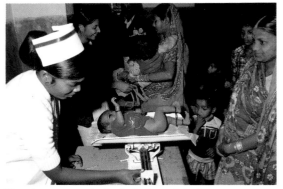

Keeping a record of a baby's weight is one way to check if it is thriving.

## WATER OF LIFE

Quite often, simply installing a good supply of clean water in a poor country can make the people there much healthier. For relatively little money it is often possible to dig a well that is not too far away from the people who will need water in that area.

## WHAT CAN MONEY BUY?

You may think that it would take a lot of money to help people in poor countries to have better health care, but in fact quite small amounts can help save lives. Think about ways in which you can give some money to help people in poor countries.

## KEEP FIT

Even if you are rich, you need to think about your own health. Here are some ideas.

Take regular exercise

Eat a balanced, healthy diet

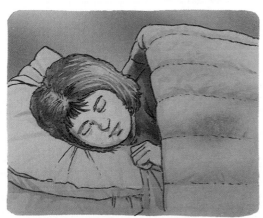

Get plenty of sleep

# FAIR SHARES FOR ALL

Only one-third of all the people in the world live in rich countries, yet they own most of the world's wealth. The people in poorer countries often want to have the same wealthy lifestyle, but the world cannot provide such luxury for everyone. The answer must be to make sure that we share things more fairly.

We all take good care of ourselves: if we really 'loved our neighbour (all our fellow human beings) as ourselves', as the Bible teaches, the world would be a fairer place.

## NEW WAYS OF LIFE FOR ALL

Many of the world's poorest people are unable to take care of their environment. They are so desperate to get food that they may take too many of the same types of crops from the land until it is worn out, or they may let animals graze it until the grass is gone and the land becomes desert.

Once, these people could have simply moved on to a new area. Now, because there are so many people in the world and because so much of the world is being used to make life pleasant for the rich, there is nowhere for them to go. Together we need to develop ways for them to use their land wisely.

## FAIR TRADE

People in the wealthy countries buy many things from poorer countries. The poor people often get a bad deal.

### Who does the packing?

A number of useful crops such as coffee, tea and sugar are grown in the poor countries of the world. The people work hard to grow and pick the crops, but then the food is shipped to rich countries to be processed and packed.

The growers get only a small amount of money for the unprocessed product, but they could get a lot more if they were allowed to do the processing and packing themselves. It might mean that these items would cost more in the shops, but poor people would have more jobs and more money.

### Bargain prices

People in rich countries can buy many goods cheaply because the people who made them were paid only a small amount of money. Fair trade would mean agreeing to pay more for some things so that the workers could have good wages. Of course, that would mean that the wealthy people would be able to afford less. . . but it would be fairer all round.

In India there is plenty of work for tea-pickers, but more jobs could be provided if processing and packing also took place locally.

People in undeveloped countries may not be able to get spare parts when machinery breaks down (left). Instead, it is better for them to use 'appropriate technology'. An example (below) is this wind-powered pump in Chile, which works well and is simple to maintain.

## THE RIGHT TOOLS FOR THE JOB

Do you know of anyone who bought a watch or a computer that was so complicated the person didn't know how to make it work? Or didn't know how to fix it when something went wrong?

People in the more industrialized countries can make all kinds of wonderful machinery: cars, farm tractors, factory equipment, and so on. The problem is that these machines are expensive to run. They are also hard to repair, and if people cannot get the right spare parts it may be impossible to get them working after they have gone wrong.

People in wealthy countries have been happy to sell this type of equipment to poor countries because they have got good money for it, but the poor people have had to spend more than they can afford and often cannot benefit from what they have.

Many people think it would be better to encourage poorer countries to use simpler hand tools that they could make and look after for themselves. It might not seem as efficient as the machinery in richer countries, but it would really work and do the job just as well.

## WHERE DOES IT COME FROM?

Go round a supermarket looking at the kinds of food you usually have in your home. Try to find out where each of the items comes from. Draw a large map of the world and draw a picture of each item in the right place.

You will probably see that many of the things you enjoy come from very far away. Try to find out about the people who supply your food, and especially try to find out if they have enough to eat.

The Bible tells us that God is just and fair. He is angry when people are greedy and do not care about others. He cares about people whom everyone else has forgotten. He cares about the wildlife he made. People who care about God should look after the creatures and people that he made. This is what the Bible says:

'I, the Lord, command you to do what is just and right. Protect the person who is being cheated from the one who is cheating him. Do not ill-treat or oppress foreigners, orphans or widows, and do not kill innocent people. . .'

'Aren't five sparrows sold for two pennies? Yet not one sparrow is forgotten by God.'

(The first quotation comes from the Old Testament, the book of the prophet Jeremiah; the second from the New Testament Gospel of Luke.)

The Bible also says that God is still in control of the world, which is a great comfort! He made a world which constantly changes, yet he knows what will happen in the future, even though we do not. He is there to help, as we try to look after it better.

## HIGH TECH, LOW TECH

Some people are so upset by the way we have used the world that they have decided to go back to a simpler way of living. They farm the land in good ways and try to live simply. At the same time they try to share what they have with others.

A group of Christians called Mennonites once decided that the simple farming life was the right way to live. Their beliefs made them very unpopular in Europe about two centuries ago, and so many of them moved to North America.

Even today, most of them live on farms. Some of them have refused to use modern technology, and they still use horses to pull farm equipment and the buggies in which they ride to church.

They do not have fancy stoves or fridges in their homes, but prepare delicious food from what they grow. Their farms are very prosperous and they often give their extra money to help people in their community or to send to people in the very poor countries.

The Mennonites set an example in earlier times, and today they point to a 'more-with-less' lifestyle that should make us think very hard about the way we live. But we cannot all go back to live on small farms — there simply isn't enough land left in the world. Whether we live in the town or country, we must learn to use the world's money better, as well as its wildlife and resources. Together, we need to find new ways to keep God's world in balance.

Contrasts in twentieth-century food production. Mennonite farmers (right) continue their traditional and successful agricultural methods, while plant technologists (left) work out how to make crops more efficient and productive.

## RICH BUT EMPTY

Rich countries have a great deal of knowledge and most of the world's money and materials. But they do not have all the answers!

Even millionaires are not always happy. A loving, caring family is more important than money, and some families in poor countries could teach richer ones some lessons!

God's love is even more important. If God made us like himself, and we have forgotten how to be friends with him, we have lost a vital part of life.

Jesus said that he is able to satisfy the needs of our hearts. That means that he can give us the things that will make us really happy, not just more things to clutter up our homes. We need to hear what God has to say to us through the Bible.

As we try to live in harmony with the natural world and with people in other countries, we need to work out a new lifestyle that will help bring us closer to God's pattern.

**People all over the world find that the Bible shows them ways to care for one another and to share what they have with others.**

# INDEX